# HENRY JAMES

## and Lamb House

Rye

The National Trust

# The Master

'It is really good enough to be a kind of little, becoming, high-door'd, brass-knocker'd *façade* to one's life.'

*Henry James on Lamb House, 1897*

Henry James was 55 when he settled at Lamb House in 1897, and had been living in Britain for more than 20 years. In novels like *Daisy Miller* (1879) and *The Portrait of a Lady* (1881), he had analysed with great psychological insight the influence of old European values upon the cosmopolitan world of American high society into which he had been born. English country house life appealed just as much to James himself, and after the humiliating failure of his play *Guy Domville* in 1895, he needed a quiet refuge from the hurly-burly of London. Lamb House provided it.

Lamb House appeared as Mr Longdon's home in James's next novel, *The Awkward Age* (1898):

> Old, square, red-roofed, well assured of its right to the place it took up in the world.... Suggestive of panelled rooms, of precious mahogany, of portraits of women dead, of coloured china glimmering through glass doors and delicate silver reflected on bared tables, the thing was one of those impressions of a particular period that it takes two centuries to produce.

It was here that James wrote his three late masterpieces, *The Wings of the Dove* (1902), *The Ambassadors* (1903) and *The Golden Bowl* (1904), which earned him his nickname, 'The Master'. His love for the 'blessed, the invaluable, little old refuge

quality of dear L.H.' only grew with the years. He particularly enjoyed showing his friends round, as the novelist Edith Wharton recalled: 'He who thought himself so detached from material things tasted the simple joys of proprietorship when, with a deprecating air, he showed his fine Georgian panelling and his ancient brick walls to admiring visitors.' Because of Lamb House, he decided to take British citizenship in 1915, the year before his death.

In his life and work, James helped Britons and Americans to understand one another. So it was apt that in 1950 his nephew's widow should give Lamb House to the National Trust 'to be preserved as an enduring symbol of the ties that unite the British and American people'.

Henry James was sculpted by F. Derwent Wood in 1913 (Tate Gallery; on loan to Lamb House)

The garden front of the house

Lamb House lies at the corner of cobbled West Street, 'the small old world street, where not one of the half-dozen wheeled vehicles of Rye ever passes'

James by the garden door of Lamb House. His secretary Theodora Bosanquet thought he looked like a Roman nobleman posing as a country gentleman

## The Lambs of Lamb House

Lamb House takes its name from the person who built it – James Lamb (1693–1756). His monument in Rye church calls him 'a man of uncommon virtue ... with the integrity of a merchant, and the courtesy of a gentleman'. Thanks to the Pelhams, one of the most influential families in Sussex, in 1714 he became Collector of Customs for Rye (then still a seaport). He also served as mayor thirteen times and managed the parliamentary constituency on behalf of the Duke of Newcastle, the most powerful of all the Pelhams. Lamb was a wine merchant, which must have helped to lubricate the elections, but it cannot have been a difficult job, as there were only 33 people in Rye entitled to vote.

In 1717 Lamb married Martha Grebell, the co-heiress to a brewery on the corner of West Street, which he pulled down five years later to build a smart new home. Lamb House is a model of early Georgian sobriety – of mottled red brick, carefully cut to make the tapering window heads and laid-in sunk panels in the parapet, which hides the dormer windows. The only decoration is to the brackets which support the hood over the unusually tall door. The large brass knocker serves as a latch inside. The interior is laid out around a panelled staircase hall with twisted balusters up the stairs. In 1743 Lamb added the Garden Room – a separate banqueting room with a bay window looking down the street. Sadly, this was destroyed in 1940, but otherwise the house has changed very little since.

Lamb House's brief moment in the limelight came in early 1726, when a storm drove George I's ship on to Camber Sands. Lamb offered his own bed to the King, although his wife was heavily pregnant. Indeed, she gave birth during the night, and as heavy snow kept the King in Rye, he agreed to be a godfather at the baptism two days later, giving a silver bowl and 100 guineas as a christening present. Not surprisingly, the Lambs called the child George.

The Lambs brought up nine children here, being succeeded by their eldest son, Thomas (1719–1804), who served as mayor of Rye no fewer than 20 times. His monument calls him 'benevolent and humane, in his manners cheerful and social, in the discharge of every duty faithful'. Thomas's son, the Rev. George Augustus Lamb, inherited in turn, but lived here only briefly, preferring to lease out the house to a succession of tenants, who are said to have included one of George IV's mistresses. The 1832 Reform Act ended the Lambs' political power in Rye, and on George Augustus's death in 1864, the house was sold to a local banker, Francis Bellingham.

The Rev. George Augustus Lamb – the last of the family to live at Lamb House

Rye in the late 19th century; James called his adopted home 'a russet Arcadia'

'There are two rooms of complete old oak – one of them a delightful little parlour.' Here hangs a portrait of George I, who stayed at Lamb House in 1726

Thomas Lamb, who owned Lamb House between 1756 and 1804; painted by Allan Ramsay in 1753 (National Gallery of Scotland, Edinburgh)

## The Great Good Place

'It is the very calmest and yet cheerfullest that I could have dreamed – in the little old, cobble-stoned, grass-grown, red-roofed town, on the summit of its mildly pyramidal hill and close to its noble old church – the chimes of which will sound sweet in my goodly old red-walled garden.'

*Henry James on Lamb House, 1897*

Henry James discovered Lamb House by accident. In 1895 he was visiting his American architect-friend Edward Warren, when he spotted a watercolour Warren had sketched of the Garden Room. Intrigued, he went to look at the house the following summer while he was staying nearby, and fell in love with it. He told his sister Alice:

> There was no appearance whatever that one could ever have it; either that its fond proprietor would give it up or that if he did it could come at all within one's means: So I simply sighed and renounced; tried to think no more about it, till at last, out of the blue, a note from the good local ironmonger, to whom I had whispered at the time my hopeless passion, informed me that by the sudden death of the owner and the preference (literal) of his son for Klondike it might perhaps drop into my lap.

And so it did. In 1897 James took out a 21-year lease: this 'most portentous parchment', as he called it, now hangs in the Entrance Hall. Two years later, he bought the freehold for £2,000. He called in Warren to supervise redecoration: 'It has been so well lived in and taken care of that – the doing – off one's own bat – is reduced mainly to sanitation and furnishing – which latter includes the peeling off of old papers from several roomfuls of pleasant top-to-toe wood panelling.' His main additions were new fireplaces with surrounds of Siena marble and old Dutch tiles, and new French windows and fitted bookcases in the Morning Room. In 1899 a fire broke out under a hearth, which entailed more repairs, although the fire brigade 'arrived with very decent promptness and operated with intelligence and tact'.

James filled Lamb House with books, Whistler etchings, Burne-Jones paintings and portraits of writers he admired like Flaubert. It became the centre of his life: 'It's astonishing how, within and without, everything wears and how, even now I discover new charm in the familiar and new assurances in the usual.'

The Garden of the Hesperides; watercolour by Miacci, which James first saw in Venice in 1854

James bought Hendrik Andersen's terracotta bust of the young Conte Bevilacqua in Rome in 1899: 'He is the first object my eyes greet in the morning and the last at night'

Henry James, painted by Philip Burne-Jones in 1894, three years before he settled at Lamb House. He shaved off his beard in 1900

This drawing of the Garden Room by Edward Warren stirred James to buy the house

# Life at Lamb House

James predicted that Lamb House offered 'every promise of yielding me an indispensable retreat from May to October'. However, if the weather was mild, he often stayed here till Christmas, before returning to his rooms in the Reform Club in London for the rest of the winter.

His daily routine varied little. He was woken about 8, had breakfast in his bedroom upstairs (known as the King's Room, since George I had slept here in 1726), came down at 9, and started work at 10. James lived in some style, but his novels were never best-sellers and he did not have substantial private means. So he had to write every day. In the summer he worked in the Garden Room, 'that stately and unexpected appendage to the unadorned cube of the house', as Edith Wharton called it. When the weather got colder, he moved upstairs to the Green Room (not open to visitors).

In 1896 rheumatism forced James to give up writing longhand; from then on, he dictated his novels to a secretary, who took down his words directly on to a typewriter: it was 'like accompanying a singer on the piano', wrote Mary Weld, who worked for him till 1904. Her successor, Theodora Bosanquet, explained that James often struggled with his convoluted prose style: 'He liked to be able to relieve the tension of a difficult sentence by a glance down the street; he enjoyed hailing a passing friend or watching a motor-car pant up the sharp little slope.' During the pauses, she read a book.

After lunch, which was often rather basic nursery fare, he would go for a walk with his dachshund, Maximilian, having selected a hat from the many that lay waiting on the table in the Hall, as H.G. Wells remembered: 'A tweed cap and stout stick for the marsh, a soft comfortable deerstalker if he were to turn aside to the golf club [James joined, not to play, but for the teas], a light-brown felt hat and a cane for a morning walk down to the harbour, a grey felt hat with a black band and a gold-headed cane of greater importance if afternoon calling in the town was afoot.' Sometimes, he would take to his bicycle, clad in knickerbockers and a startlingly bright check jacket. As James got older and stouter, he became more sedentary. He never owned a car, but loved motoring, often going off on jaunts with Edith Wharton to romantic spots like Bodiam Castle: 'For a long time no one spoke; then James turned to me and said solemnly: "Summer afternoon – summer afternoon; to me those have always been the two most beautiful words in the English language."'

In the evening, if there were no guests, James would sit up revising what he had dictated that morning – getting his secretary to stay late with cups of tea and chocolate. They worked by lamplight (there was no electricity), but James was one of the first people to have a telephone, which he kept in the room to the right of the Hall.

Although James was a bachelor, he had an indoor staff of four, who slept on the top floor: cook, parlourmaid, housemaid and a valet butler – firstly, Smith, who took to drink, and then the devoted Burgess Noakes, who was bantamweight boxing champion of Sussex. James called him 'my gnome Burgess'; Noakes called James 'the old toff'.

James standing by the door to the garden

The Garden Room, which James 'laughingly called the temple of the Muse [according to an American visitor]. This is his own place *par excellence*. A good writing table and one for his secretary, a typewriter, books and a sketch by du Maurier, with a few other pictures (rather mementoes than works of art), excellent windows with clear light – such is the temple!'

The Entrance Hall: 'the place has been carefully done up, and is very clean, trim, precise, but all old and harmonious' (A.C. Benson, 1900)

# Taking tea with Henry James

'Under certain circumstances there are few hours in life more agreeable than the hour dedicated to the ceremony known as afternoon tea.'

The opening sentence of *The Portrait of a Lady* (1881)

James in the garden in 1901

The Green Room, James's upstairs study, in 1912

The Morning Room in 1912

The locals took pride in having such a distinguished author living in their midst and respected his privacy. James got on well with his neighbours, but sometimes pined for the stimulation of London society. He made up for this by receiving numerous literary visitors, many of whom settled in this part of England and became friends. There was H.G. Wells at Sandgate, Joseph Conrad at Pent Farm near Hythe, Stephen Crane at Brede Place, Rudyard Kipling at Burwash, and Ford Madox Hueffer at Winchelsea. 'A ring of conspirators' is what Wells called the group.

James usually met his visitors at Rye station with his gardener, who would push their luggage up the hill in a wheelbarrow. A particularly welcome guest was Edith Wharton, who would arrive at the front door in her car:

There he stood on the doorstep, the white-panelled hall with its old prints and crowded book-cases forming a background to his heavy loosely-clothed figure. Arms out-stretched, lips and eyes twinkling, he came down to the car, uttering cries of mock amazement and mock humility at the undeserved honour of my visit.

The literary critic Desmond MacCarthy described a visit in 1914 near the end of James's life:

He was sitting in an armchair with a foot-rest. His eyes half-shut. He seemed to speak with difficulty as though whenever his lips closed, they stuck together, and the wheels of his mind turned with a ponderous smooth difficulty, as though there was not steam enough to move so large an engine. He asked me not to smoke and rang for tea, which when it arrived he eyed with envy. 'If I take tea it will either kill me or do me good, what shall I do?' I said the decision was too momentous for me to make. He decided not to take tea. The conversation laboured through a heavy sea. I sometimes thought it would never climb the next wave of silence. Gradually I became aware, however, that we were making progress. We began to talk about the power to visualize memories and imaginary scenes. He seemed to think that a novelist's power depended upon it. I admitted that in his own case the dependance was marked, but in that of others was not the ocular nerve of the reader often positively starved?... Then we went through the novelists with this idea in our heads, and he read to me. All the time he was getting brisker and brisker, till at last from a semi-comatose condition he began to grow positively lively – shovelling on coal and eating absently cold tea cake and sweet buns.

James walking in the garden with the novelist Mrs Humphry Ward, who remembered 'the smooth-shaven, finely-cut face, now alive with talk and laughter, now shrewdly, one might say coldly observant; the face of a satirist – but so human! – so alive to all that under-world of destiny through which move the weaknesses of men and women'

## The Garden

Henry James was not a gardener: 'I am *densely* ignorant – only just barely know dahlias from mignonette', he admitted in 1898. So when he took on Lamb House, he asked his friend Alfred Parsons for advice:

> Best of men as well as best of landscape-painters-and-decorators, [Parsons] went down with me and revealed to me the most charming possibilities for the treatment of the tiny out-of-door part – it amounts to about an acre of garden and lawn, all shut in by the peaceful old red wall aforesaid, on which the most flourishing old espaliers, apricots, pears, plums and figs, assiduously grow. It appears that it's a glorious little growing exposure, air and soil – and all the things that were still flourishing out of doors (November 20) were a joy to behold.

Parsons recommended planting a walnut tree and laying out a new lawn and paths, surrounded by box-edged borders filled with crocuses, tulips and hyacinths. Lupins, fuchsias and geraniums filled another bed, a large greenhouse (now gone) contained vines, and there was a huge *Campsis radicans*. James left the work to his gardener, George Gammon, 'an excellent, quiet, trustworthy fellow in all respects'. As Miss Bosanquet recalled, 'It never failed to give the owner pleasure to look out of this convenient window [of the Garden Room] at his English garden where he could watch

Gabriel, E.F. Benson's gardener, mowing the lawn. His care for the garden was so great that Benson felt like a guest in his presence

Henry James and E.F. Benson remembered their beloved dogs with these tombstones in the garden

his English gardener digging the flower-beds or mowing the lawn or sweeping up fallen leaves.' Gammon won numerous prizes at that most English of institutions – the local flower show, and the Anglophile James revelled in the reflected glory.

Despite the high walls, the garden sits at the top of the town exposed to sea gales, which brought down Parsons's walnut and an ancient mulberry, to James's distress: 'It's very sad, for he was the making of the garden – he was *it* in person'.

The garden today still delights the eye. The flamboyant *Campsis* beloved by James clings to the garden wall as it always did, but is now joined by other climbers – jasmine, roses and *Trachelospermum*. The lawn, the largest within the citadel of Rye, is bordered by beds containing spring bulbs, roses, lavender, day-lilies and other herbaceous varieties to ensure continuous interest throughout the year. The border beyond the lawn is filled with evergreen trees and shrubs and leads to the small secluded area in the far corner where you can find the graves of James's dogs.

A path leads through a trelliswork screen, against which apple trees are trained. Here you come on a small round pond surrounded with paving and rose beds. Beyond is James's kitchen garden with its herbs, soft fruit and vegetables, all protected by the mellow brick walls he held in such affection.

Topiary flanks a Victorian cast-iron seat in the garden

The *Campsis radicans* is one of the few plants in the garden known to have survived from James's time

An early view of the garden front

# E.F. Benson

James never married, and so on his death in 1916 bequeathed the house to his nephew, Henry James junior, who let it to a series of tenants. The writer E.F. Benson, a friend of James who had first visited Lamb House in 1900, took over the lease in 1919. A bachelor like James, he shared the house for awhile with his brother, A.C. Benson, the Master of Magdalene College, Cambridge, who stayed during the university vacations. After his brother's death in 1925, E.F. Benson lived here all the year round, bird-watching, playing chess or cards with neighbours, or picking out the Moonlight Sonata on his Bechstein grand in the Garden Room. Outside, he turned a neglected corner into the Secret Garden, in which a marble bust of the Emperor Augustus was surrounded by forget-me-nots, Darwin tulips, scarlet anemones and aubretia, while *Clematis × jackmanii* and *microphylla* 'Miss Bateman' and Mermaid roses covered the enclosing walls. On sunny days, Benson would sit here reading or writing.

Benson was an even more prolific author than James, regularly turning out 2,000 words a day: 'A writer is not someone who *can* write, but someone who *does* write.' Most of his more than 70 books are now forgotten, but not the six *Mapp and Lucia* novels, which were directly inspired by Lamb House and by Rye society:

> I had seen the ladies of Rye [called Tilling in the books] doing their shopping in the High Street every morning, carrying large market baskets, and bumping into one another in narrow doorways and talking in a very animated fashion.... I outlined an elderly atrocious spinster and established her in Lamb House [called Mallards]. She should be the centre of social life abhorred and dominant, and she should sit like a giant spider behind the curtains of the Garden Room, spying on her friends, and I knew that her name must be Elizabeth Mapp.

Despite the acid picture of Rye painted in the *Mapp and Lucia* books, Benson was made mayor of the town in 1934–7, like so many of his predecessors at Lamb House. And it was in the nearby churchyard that he was buried in 1940.

E.F. Benson with Taffy in the early 1930s

Benson welcoming Queen Mary to Lamb House in 1935 after having taken her round the Rye antique shops

(*Far left*) Benson in the Secret Garden he created from an overgrown plot behind the house: he called it 'an outdoor sitting-room'. The bust of the Roman Emperor Augustus came from a local shop

## Recent Years

In 1940 a German bomb demolished the Garden Room and destroyed most of its contents, including almost 200 books from James's library and Benson's piano, which ended up hanging from the telephone wires outside. The house itself survived, but was left uninhabitable for the rest of the war, and in the austere post-war world it was impossible to rebuild the Garden Room: a plaque set into the outside wall marks where it once stood.

In 1950 Henry James junior's widow Dorothy presented Lamb House to the National Trust. Alas, it came without its surviving contents, which were sold in May 1949 and are now scattered across the world. The Trust has gradually been retrieving mementoes of Henry James's life, with the help of a succession of distinguished tenants, who have included the biographer H. Montgomery Hyde, Rumer Godden, author of *Black Narcissus*, and Sir Brian Batsford, designer of the distinctive dust jackets to so many Batsford travel books of the 1930s.

Lamb House in the snow; a Christmas card painted by a former tenant, Sir Brian Batsford, showing the Garden Room destroyed in 1940